Reading this book i
you spiritually. It
applications that ca
If you want to devel
guide.

*Carolyn Draper*
*Primary school teacher*

Jenny Campbell is such a good connector. She connects deep theology to everyday life, the past to the present, the mysterious to the meaningful, the challenges to the opportunities, our doing to our being and, most importantly, the work of the Spirit of God to ordinary people like you and me. This book will help you to keep in step with the Spirit as you give time and space to draw near to God and seek his presence to enrich you and form you into his likeness.

*Revd Canon Tim Montgomery*
*Missional Leadership Development Officer,*
*Diocese of Liverpool*

This little book of wisdom is for anyone; for the seeker of spiritual direction in Christ it is invaluable.

*Andy Packer*
*Retired headteacher and seeker of answers*

*Strengthen Your Core* packs a lot into a small book. As an octogenarian wishing to have read the book earlier, it is still a relief to understand now, that our

LORD intended the Beatitudes to be a goal to reach for rather than, as Campbell illustrates with refreshing humour and empathising self-deprecation, being perfect now. The comparison between the struggle of the Ancient Greek athlete and that of the Christian spiritual athlete gives form and structure to spiritual gymnastics. It is never too late to have a go.

*Suzy Miles*
*Octogenarian and artist*

*Strengthen Your Core* is an insightful, easy to understand, practical book to strengthen your spiritual muscles at any stage of your faith. It is perfect for anybody who wants a concise, practical guide to take their discipleship to the next level! I would recommend this for anyone wanting to strengthen their faith for their independence as a Christian.

*Matt Human*
*A-Level student*

# STRENGTHEN
## YOUR CORE

**PRACTICAL
SPIRITUAL FORMATION
FOR EVERY DAY**

**JENNY CAMPBELL**

# CONTENTS

# INTRODUCTION

The cancellation of the 2020 Olympic Games came as a shock. For over a century, every four years, this global battle of champions has gripped and enthralled us. From 776 BC in Ancient Greece, when Herakles called for a thanksgiving after war in honour of the chief Greek god Zeus, and for a thousand years every four years, the games were the supreme sporting challenge. The Greek philosopher Socrates (470–399 BC) put forward the idea that the training school or gymnasium, *gymnastikē* (literally the place of nakedness as athletes competed completely naked), developed not only the body, but also the soul (*Republic* 376e).

Let's take this idea of the development of the soul through physical training with self-discipline, mental toughness, endurance and courage built into the programme. Now, let's apply that thought to Christian spiritual discipline, some of which is outwardly physical and all of which is inwardly spiritual. We must, of course, allow for the fact that Christian excellence is not measured by the Greek standards of the body beautiful. Working out in the gymnasium was designed to fashion the body magnificent. The Christian has an altogether different goal, of being fashioned into the magnificence of Jesus Christ, into his image. We want to look like Jesus rather than a Greek god! If there are physical benefits they will be secondary to the greater cause of the likeness of Christ.

Greek boys trained with coaches in schools and athletic grounds. Christians need coaches too and the purpose of this book is to show how we can get fit with the help of the Holy Spirit and, at times, another person or group of people. We call this process 'spiritual direction'. *Hold on! I thought that was only for vicars and 'holy' people?* Not at all. Spiritual direction is a practice going all the way back to the Early Church. In the first instance, Christians are dependent upon the Holy Spirit to guide and direct them. However, anyone seeking a more rounded and grounded way of life may consult a priest, minister or respected godly person. In this book we shall be looking at both these ways: being directed by God alone and being directed by God with another person's help. First, let's establish a training regime.

Just as the Greek athlete learned skills for the

contest, the Church has a set of tools called the spiritual disciplines. *Oh, that's just tradition, that belongs to the musty, fusty old Church. We don't need them today. We are free of tradition, free of the law!* But we *do* need them if we are to avoid becoming a spineless, anything-goes kind of Church. If we are to become like Jesus then we need to do what he did – and he exercised every single one of the spiritual disciplines. Jesus was spiritually fit!

*Well then, what are they?* They are eight significant disciplines, which any denomination can sign up to:

- Reading Scripture
- Silence
- Prayer
- Fasting
- Anointing oil for confession and healing
- Pilgrimage
- Gifts of money and service
- Worship and celebration

So how about we have someone walking alongside us as we practise one or other of these disciplines, someone to hold us accountable, to inspire and encourage us, at times to adjust the direction slightly? That's the first step – a training regime.

I remember working, fresh out of theological college, as a member of staff in a parish, not only full-time but full of what I knew and how clever I was – at everything. I soon discovered that the *real* movers and shakers in the congregation were completely intentional about their daily prayers and Bible reading, about worship, about fasting and generally everything I had been taught and adhered to – in my mind. One by one these astonishing people held up for me a mirror of the good Christian life in the power of the Holy Spirit, and, by their lives and practices, showed me a path of spiritual discipline. One of them had the courage to tell me that she simply could not listen to another word I preached until she saw that my words reflected my life! That is a wake-up call and true accountability and it not only set me straight but also directed me to seek the LORD's help and to be changed.

The second step is the method. How shall we do this? We need something to get us going, something extra, something to spur us on our way. We turn to the Beatitudes, arguably one of the greatest teachings ever, but seemingly completely unobtainable by mere mortals. These eight sayings of Jesus Christ, recorded in Matthew 5:1–12, include the following areas:

- Poverty
- Mourning
- Humility
- Hunger for righteousness
- Mercy
- Purity
- Being a peacemaker
- Being persecuted

How would we go about exercising such unworldly attributes? And how would we test our progress in a state of blessedness? For blessedness, a rather quaint way of describing happiness, would be our goal in 'working out' in the Beatitudes. (*Beatitudo*, the Latin noun, is the state of being prosperous, rich, well-off, abundant and happy.) And so it is: 'How blessed, how excessively over the top, abundantly happy are the poor, meek, reviled...'

I remember arriving at Banjul airport in The Gambia in West Africa for a short mission trip. My young companion and I waited for hours in growing frustration and agitation for our hosts. And then, finally they came, car horns blowing, people singing and waving banners of welcome in triumphal procession – the children of the Banjul Jesus Ministry with their leaders. We felt so honoured, much loved and wholly blessed by these little people – small the eyes of the world but great in joy, excitement and happiness, and in the eyes of God.

The third step is the exercise itself. For this we need rungs on the ladder, notches to mark our chart. In this guide, we will bring together one spiritual discipline and one beatitude, eight pairs. We will do this in eight exercise Workouts, one for each of the pairs, logging our attempts as we go along. For example, working out in reading Scripture and watching how spiritual richness and prosperity replace poverty of spirit or material goods.

At the end of each Workout I invite you to think and pray about the 'who' part of the exercise. Who is it who will walk with us? Will we rely largely on the Helper, the Holy Spirit, to manage our lives? Will we invite someone to walk with us informally, a friend or a prayer triplet, for example, or will we seek out a specially designated person to see us through on a more formal arrangement?

*This all seems a bit like hard work, a bit of an effort!* Well, a boot camp is not for the fainthearted. Jesus took his disciples up a mountain to give those learners this hard teaching. These were the hardcore, not the curious crowd. He 'sat down'

(Matt. 5:1) in the custom of the Jewish rabbi teacher and 'opened His mouth' (v2, NKJV) – a technical term meaning that something of real importance was about to be delivered. Are you ready for the Jesus challenge? I invite you into the school, on to the circuit, on to the athletic grounds. The benefits are beatific and out of this world!

# WORKOUT ONE

## Poor in spirit and rich in Scripture

As a tutor, I teach students how to read for an assignment during student induction week. Reading, for some, is a struggle and a hard task; for others, easy-peasy. You probably have some hazy recollection of learning to read at school. To conquer language, to enter the world of others, of ideas, of stories, of thought – what an achievement for a young one. Similarly, a Christian in a school of discipleship begins with a book. The Bible is, in fact, a library of books to be understood and absorbed, to enter into the world of God – his thoughts, his ideas.

I'm in no doubt that the majority of Christians would like to improve in their reading and hearing of Scripture. Many of us are slow Bible readers and learners, others seem deft and swift-footed, leaping the rocky paths of difficult passages with speed and alacrity. We envy these athletes of the Word. How can we train ourselves to be better at disciplined reading (or hearing in our audio age)? These feelings of poor Bible knowledge and application are an excellent start as we begin our Workout with the first beatitude, as it has everything to do with poverty of spirit.

## First beatitude

Jesus said, 'Blessed are the poor in spirit, for theirs is the kingdom of heaven' (Matt. 5:3). To be poor in spirit, and to sense that poverty, is precisely the start of a new journey in delving into the Bible, into the riches of the kingdom of heaven. Poor in spirit and rich in Scripture. To be unsatisfied and empty-handed as we read is the best way to be fed. It is easier to receive satisfying soul-food without preconceived ideas or too many analytical tools. It is easier for the LORD to teach us when our minds lie fallow. At this you may protest: *Oh no, I'm not losing my intellect at the expense of simplicity, thank you very much. I'm not about to bury my brain.* Or, you may argue: *I already know this, I do that already, I read every day and I wait for the Lord to speak.*

These objections are completely understand-able. God gave us minds not to abandon but to use when engaging with Scripture. Absolutely. And many can testify to Bibles chock-full with notes in the margins, written while reading devotionally. Some never give up their old, tattered Bibles because they treasure these notes. However, it is always helpful to be on the lookout for ways to strengthen and sharpen our hearing and seeing. One of these ways is an ancient practice of prayerful contemplation of the text called the *Lectio Divina*.

## Lectio Divina

This method is a refreshing means to reading Scripture and a wonderful well of enlightenment. The phrase comes from the Latin: *lectio* (noun) the act of reading, *divina* (adjective) divine, prophetic (think of divining water). And so we have 'divine reading' or, even more exciting perhaps, 'prophetic reading'. I like to think of this exercise as a foreseeing kind of reading (not in the sense of fortune telling), a reading that seeks to draw out the prophetical sense, a kind of higher spiritual meaning, looking for hidden gems in the depths of Scripture. It is almost as though deeply embedded in the lines of text, written millennia ago, are solutions to the complexities, questions and puzzlements that confront Christians every day.

This uncovering, this revealing, this revelation is by, through and in the Spirit of God, who is the inspirer of Scripture. And it is this partnership with the Holy Spirit that puts spiritual direction right at the forefront in the exercise of the *Lectio Divina*. As we cooperate deliberately with the Holy Spirit in our reading, we open a door to divine guidance more readily than if we approached the text as a piece of writing detached from God and up to us to decipher. Clearly, we all seek intelligible perspective on our lives and the lives of others, and we need unambiguous direction as we pray for the government, our nation and the welfare of other nations. A divine reading gives our prayers weight.

## Jesus

To spur us on, let us consider Jesus. The New Testament shows us that Jesus Christ was a man who knew the Word of God. Luke's Gospel tells us that Jesus, as a youngster, astounded his listeners in the Jerusalem Temple with his understanding of the Hebrew scriptures (2:46–47). Later on, Luke describes Jesus at war with Satan in the desert. As the tempter offers the fasting Son of God food, wealth, prestige and kingdoms, the rebuttals are driven home with sharp retorts straight out of the Hebrew scriptures: 'Man shall not live on bread alone', 'Worship the LORD your God and serve him only', 'Do not put the LORD your God to the test' (4:1–13).

Following this titanic struggle, Luke then shows Jesus as a young adult in his local synagogue of Nazareth, handling the Hebrew scriptures set for that Sabbath with prophetic insight, pleasing his hearers with his preaching until he angers the congregation and only just escapes their rage and murderous intent (4:16–30). Jesus knew his Jewish scriptures and used them well, and we are to know and use well those same Old Testament scriptures. In addition, we have the new scriptures, the New Testament, written because of Jesus Christ. We are to use the entire Bible as a sword and we need to get busy practising how to wield it as successfully as the Master.

## Benefits

Psalm 1 describes the position of one who takes pleasure in the Scriptures, one who meditates, ruminating on the Word, much like a cow chewing, day and night:

*Blessed is the one*
*who does not walk in step with the wicked*
*or stand in the way that sinners take*

> *or sits in the company of mockers,*
> *but whose delight is in the law of the* LORD,
> *and who meditates on his law day and night.*
> *That person is like a tree*
> *planted by streams of water,*
> *which yields its fruit in season*
> *and whose leaf does not wither –*
> *whatever they do prospers.*
>
> (PSA. 1:1–3)

Wrestling a particularly bad bout of depression as a 30-year-old postgraduate student, I immersed myself in the study of Greek and the Bible. I would read a passage from the New Testament each morning (in English!) in the way described above. This slow labour dug up a daily dose of divine remedy: a phrase, a line, a word would stick, and the repetition of that word over and over again became a kind of mantra, a lifeline, which invigorated my soul and gave impetus for prayer. Like fragrant flowers these daily words became a bouquet by the end of each week. But more than comfort, I discovered a weapon of war and, over the next months, my drooping spirit revived to fight off the darkness. I have never returned to that pit of despair.

In that slough of despond, I learned that

exercise in secret is preparation for the warfront, for the battle for the soul. And that this regime is akin to a Greek athlete whose development in the expertise of javelin, discus, running, boxing and so on, were skills honed for the handling of weapons, so that each citizen was ready to serve his city at a time of war. Christians are citizens of heaven whose fight is not against flesh and blood but against a deadly enemy of God and of his people (Eph. 6:12). Let's always be ready to pick up the sword of the Spirit, the Word of God (Eph. 6:17).

## Who will go with me?

To enjoy the plain meaning of Scripture is the result of regularly listening to sermons and talks, be they live or online podcasts or YouTube videos. We develop a habit of imbibing, of taking in information. In this process we are reliant upon the Holy Spirit in the speaker to convey the message and we may indeed receive guidance for our lives from time to time. It is unlikely that we will spend much time offloading to another what we have heard, unless there is something worrying in the message given – there simply isn't time.

In the method of the *Lectio Divina* outlined

above, there is a gradual drip feed of truth into our souls by the Spirit of God. Any interpretation comes slowly and quietly through the words of the Bible passage and not through any single person. In this case, we are wholly dependent on the Holy Spirit's direction. And this is very good for us, especially for those who prefer to sit at the feet of their favourite Bible teacher or preacher rather than grapple with Scripture themselves.

This is not to say that one to one discussion with a friend or spiritual director about a baffling text is wrong. Nor that receiving a word from the New or Old Testaments given by a fellow Christian, which proves pertinent to one's life at the time, is not helpful. In our pursuit of the study of Scripture, however, there is little substitute for a download by the LORD of personal revelation, straight down from heaven as it were, as we settle to Scripture ourselves. If this is the case, how then shall we go about it?

## Working out in Scripture

As the *Lectio Divina* goes all the way back to the Early Church, we are recovering what is a very old piece of spiritual treasure and, as with something from another era, it may take some getting used to in its unfamiliarity. Persevere!

## ▷ Step one

First comes the act of reading itself. For ease of transmission, probably a hard copy of the Bible is better than a tablet, phone or computer. Select a passage from either the New or Old Testaments: a psalm, a parable, a short drama or story, a prophecy or wise saying. Settle down comfortably and pray a prayer to the Holy Spirit to inspire your reading. Now begin to read out loud or audibly under the breath – in itself a physical and muscular effort. In your breath, there is some sort of connection with the Spirit who *is* breath or wind, *pneuma* (Greek) and *ruach* (Hebrew). It is almost as though in our physical breath, in this exercise, we come to rely on the breath of God, the Spirit who inspires us and the Bible, as we read.

Read very slowly, deliberately and deeply, paying close attention to the page. As your eyes travel over the words and your ears listen to their sounds, permit your spirit and heart to reach out for their meaning. Read the text again, slowly and contemplatively, and a third time. Then rest. Wait and then, if helpful, write down what you see in your mind's eye or hear in your spirit. You may land on a single word, be struck by a phrase, get stuck on an idea or absorbed in a thought. If nothing is evident, leave it and go your way.

### Step two

The next day, practise the exercise on the same passage or a different one. Repeat the reading exercise for several days. As with physical exercise, our strenuous exertions take a while to kick in and deliver dividends. We need to keep at it.

### Step three

Now comes the shaping of a workout regime, so that it becomes a habit. Over time, a regular disciplined reading will start to form part of a rhythm of life to concentrate the mind. Slow down and let the prophetic meaning in the text emerge. What does this mean for you? How is this word nourishing your spirit? Let the word linger, speak it, learn it, memorise it, write it out, have it on the fridge door. More than food is God's Word. Have the Word to hand in time of need, in turmoil, in distress, in worry or anxiety, in flatness and in fortitude.

We are told to 'gird up the loins of your mind' (NKJV), in other words to have 'minds that are alert and fully sober' (1 Pet. 1:13). The practice of the *Lectio Divina* lifts the mind to God and his glory, and if we are made miserable by what we read we can repent and turn to him for help. The main thing is to keep doing the main thing: looking out for blessings as rich treasure is revealed from the Word of God.

# WORKOUT TWO

## Grief-stricken in silence

Silence – and grief. I write this Workout at a particularly poignant moment in our world: the pandemic of COVID-19. The relentless virus is no respecter of persons and many of us are mourning losses: the death of a friend, colleague, elderly person or partner; the death of a pet or a business or a family holiday; the deprivation of hugs and cuddles with friends and family; missing seeing people in other countries or the camaraderie of work colleagues. Perhaps most profoundly we have experienced the curtailing of personal liberty, the freedom to choose, to go where and how we please.

I felt acutely the curbing of my independence at the beginning of the national lockdown when my flight to Cape Town was cancelled and the prospect of attending to my ailing, aged mother was relegated to the never-never. This anxiety carved out a hollow emptiness in my soul, a feeling I kept firmly under lock and key while working online from home. However, at the start of the holiday season, that awkward internal discomfort inconveniently poked its head above the surface of my subconscious – an unwelcome intrusion. I stared this visitor in the face and was overcome with grief.

For a few days, I mourned in silence alone, unable to express the core of my sorrow to anyone. But the LORD knew and threw a blanket of solace over me in the form of friends who came alongside and appeared to understand the inexpressible. Despite the extraordinary circumstances, a feeling of unusual happiness, of what I might call 'blessedness', came upon me – and has remained.

## Second beatitude

It is the second beatitude that has the promise of divine aid in grief. 'Blessed are those who mourn, for they will be comforted' (Matt. 5:4). During the global pandemic and its fallout, we have seen grief turn up in many guises. It is interesting that the Greek verb *penthein* (to mourn), from which *penthountes* (the ones who mourn) is used of the merchants who mourn the fall of Babylon and their loss of business: 'The merchants of the earth will weep and mourn over her because no one buys their cargoes any more' (Rev. 18:11). It is also fascinating to note that the Greek verb *parakalein* (to comfort) is sometimes used as a title for the Holy Spirit *paraklētos* (the one who comes alongside, the Comforter). In this beatitude we have the assurance of God's help – the Helper, the Consoler and Encourager – to urge and cheer up the saints. How shall we receive such strengthening in the midst of sadness? We come to our second exercise, the discipline of silence.

## Silence in retreat

We live in a noisy world. This was brought home recently in a college library – by agreed convention generally a silent place for study. The man at the desk with headphones talked very loudly and without stopping into his mobile phone about a problem at home with the gas. His conversation filled the air and prevented thought. My intervention brought a look of utter fury and annoyance and extremely reluctant compliance with my request that he speak outside the room.

Human cacophony has eclipsed silence. Even as I type this, I cannot hear the birdsong, or the wind in the tall trees. The thump, thump of drums from the teenager's room down the lane and the carpenter's piercing drill steal the silence. I find headphones to drown out the sound with more sound in my ears. Then there are aeroplanes overhead. We associate silence with flight. We run from silence. Silence is strange and unmanageable and we manage our lives to avoid it. So we speak a lot and are loud in our thoughts to block out unwanted intruders, and rough ride over the unpleasant. We believe it is better to escape grief by burying ourselves in distractions, building a big barricade over our emotions.

Silence was the commodity the adventurous hermits sought during the third century in the great trek to the Scetes desert of Egypt. These spiritually aware folk were propelled by a deeply felt sorrow for sin, drowned out in the noisy hustle and bustle of the towns and cities. The flight to the vast desert, to the caves and mountains was more precisely not a flight *from* but a flight *to*, not fleeing life but facing sin, pain, loss of faith, and fighting the inner demons. They were enclosed by silence, immersed in the self and its frailty, yet empowered to battle temptation and strengthened to follow Christ – the recipe for a happy life.

Word got out about a certain 'wisdom of the desert' and people seeking counsel journeyed from the cities to these Desert Fathers and Mothers. Some remained for a while, others went back refreshed and restored by a word from God. Can I become emotionally fit by emulating these worthies and pursuing the gift of silence? Can I imitate their lifestyle by introducing one or two principles from the desert silence and improve my quality of life?

## Jesus

We do not need to look far for a role model for the silent desert adventure. Jesus Christ went there and we are to follow in his footsteps. But he went there not once only – the famous 40 days in the wilderness battle with the devil we referred to in the previous Workout – but every day. The Gospel account is clear: Jesus left the house early before dawn and went outside, or up a mountain to pray (Mark 1:35; Luke 6:12; 11:1). In silence, the Son of God prepared himself for work that day.

## Benefits

There is a great little story in the book of Nehemiah that shows how prayer from a place of sadness can alter circumstances, and on a grand scale. Nehemiah is a Jewish exile in Persia (modern day Iran) and cupbearer to King Artaxerxes, who asks him one day why his countenance has fallen. This was the Hebrew way of enquiring: Why are you so sad? Your face tells me a story. Nehemiah has been sorrowing and sighing, fasting and praying for many days, upset by the plight of his fellow Jews and the state of the broken-down walls of Jerusalem. Who can he tell? No one. Only Yahweh his God. Yet his face tells the story, and when the king extracts the truth, he sends his cupbearer on a journey with his kingly blessing and resources to put matters right and to rebuild the walls of the city of Jerusalem. You can read all about this expedition and rebuilding in the book of Nehemiah.

## Who will go with me?

Many of us are not used to being silent as we live our lives on the trot, managing crises and people. Cultivating times of quiet requires guidance. A close friend or partner on our case will not only help us to make time for God, to be in his presence and at times to sort ourselves out, but will check up on us. And this is good news. We need to give someone the freedom to say, 'Hold on, when did you last get with God? Your absence from him is beginning to show in your life.' This kind of accountability is more often than not in the remit of a person who lives with us or who is closely involved in our life and is walking in agreement with us.

You may choose to find a spiritual director on a formal basis. You open your heart to this person, discussing the difficulty you have with being alone, or being quiet, and waiting for their wisdom on the matter. They may set you an exercise as Metropolitan Anthony Bloom (1914–2003) did for a woman who found it difficult to pray. The Russian Orthodox leader told her to go home, sit in her living room with her knitting and become aware of the silence. She did so for a time, gradually becoming aware of the LORD with her and beginning to converse with him.

Avoiding pain is the worst kind of spiritual direction we can give ourselves. The true spiritual guide will counsel us to confront the aloneness of melancholy, to go towards and not away from the loneliness of our trials and tribulations. The good spiritual friend will give us a chance to stay alone with our experience, to get in touch with our innermost self. The best spiritual direction will persuade us to take courage in both hands and risk entering that silence where we are free to listen to our hearts.

And last but not least, when all human help fails us and falls short, we have the blessed Holy Spirit, the divine Comforter, who shows up when we least expect it and throws over our mourning and grief a mantle of praise. How does this work in practice? There are many ways for the interruptions of the Spirit of God.

One such experience comes to mind. As a very 'hurt by people in church' twenty-something, I stood in a queue at the ladies' loos in a conference behind an unobtrusive woman. Yet I knew she was a songwriter of world significance and that her songs came out of her life lived in community with her US church. She turned in the queue to speak to me with such love that I welled up and blurted out my story. 'That must have been very hard for you' was all she said. Yet, at that moment, held ever so quietly in a stranger's compassionate hug, I felt my grief subside and healing came suddenly and unexpectedly.

## Working out in a desert retreat

▷ **Step one**

Let's begin with the most strenuous form of retreat. Equivalent journeys to the desert in our contemporary way of life could be an escape by

air, land or sea to a place: a pod, a caravan, a
hut, an estate, a lodge, a retreat house far away
from human beings. These flights could be on
one's own or with a close friend, partner or small
group of like-minded seekers. We can choose to
be informal or book into a guided retreat with
a spiritual advisor. If they happen at all, these
self-imposed times of exile will probably be a bit
hit and miss.

### ▷ Step two

Build into your life a regular routine of days of
refuge. These will be a day or days earmarked
during the year (much as you would a holiday)
when you retreat to a place separate from home
or work in order to hear the LORD more clearly
than you would when surrounded by people and
busyness. You can do this alone or with a group.
It's entirely up to you. The key idea, however, is to
have times of silence as part of your retreat. In my
experience as a retreat leader, I have found that
it is these moments rather than the chatty times
when the tears and fears and breakthroughs
come.

### ▷ Step three

Book in days away but do not wholly rely on

them. Building up to such an event where your whole life has to be dealt with in a very short time space of time can be quite stressful. Far better to enjoy a habit of silence every day or every few days where there is an inward journey within the soul to sort things out. Try to carve out weekly times of silence but be assured, this desire will be contested. Everything possible will contrive to stop you. Persevere! Seek out your inner space with the Holy Spirit and grapple with your opponent – your mood or affliction – and overcome with the power of Christ.

# WORKOUT THREE

## Prayerful submission
## to the mission

We remind ourselves that the Greek athletes performed their feats, after victory in war, as thanksgivings to their chief god, Zeus. They offered up their beautifully toned and sculpted bodies as sacrifices, as triumphant paeans of praise. And of course there were gains in the winner's crown of laurel, in the adulation of crowds and the exultation of their names in the halls of sporting fame – all these the fruits of disciplined training.

The Christian expression of relationship with God is not dissimilar. Christians demonstrate their allegiance to Jesus Christ by performing their thanksgivings in prayer – privately and together with others – by offering their sacrifices of praise to the LORD and their bodies as living sacrifices to his service (Heb. 13:15; Rom. 12:1). For such dedication there is the promise of a prize, a crown of life (James 1:12; Rev. 2:10), the crowd of witnesses cheering them on (Heb. 12:1) and a new name (Rev. 2:17).

A rigorous attention to prayer is the one essential element upon which all spiritual direction is agreed. Prayer is a life force: breath to the soul and vitality to the body. Without prayer, we shrivel, our souls shrinking in the supernatural, grow fat in the natural, plumped up by the ways of the world. Without prayer, we have very little spiritual vision, only our own limited ideas and inspirations. But with prayer, our small kingdoms are dwarfed by God's ultimate goals. Therefore, the inner attitude of prayer must be submission: only the meek and yielding will place life's desires and wishes in the lap of God. In this bending of the will, our earthly longings are enlarged, made new and divinised: God shares his hope for the earth with us, its inheritors. This mindset brings us to our Workout incentive, to the stimulant to activate and exercise prayer.

## Third beatitude

'Blessed are the meek, for they will inherit the earth' (Matt. 5:5). At first glance, we may cry indignantly: What nonsense is this? What on earth did Jesus mean? How can you inherit the earth when everyone knows that being an acquiescent doormat will get you nowhere? You will be trodden on, hurt and deceived.

Did Jesus get it wrong? Far from it. Being a Jewish teacher steeped in the old writings (as we have seen in his battle in the desert), Jesus based this teaching on Psalm 37:11: 'But the meek will inherit the land and enjoy peace and prosperity'. In the Hebrew Old Testament, the 'meek' are the *ani*, the poor, the humble, the lowly and the pious, oppressed by the rich and powerful and afflicted by other nations. Yet we read that Yahweh always has compassion on these little ones, saving, delivering, granting divine favour and peace in their inheritance. And the promise from Yahweh and his reward is substantial: 'to drive out before you nations greater and stronger than you and to bring you into their land to give it to you for your inheritance, as it is today' (Deut. 4:38).

In the beatitude, the Greek noun is *praus* or *praos* meaning 'mild, gentle or meek'. The Latin translation of this text has the adjective *mitis*, used of soft fruit 'mellow, mild, gentle'. The sense of true meekness, this compliant inner attitude is that of a powerful horse under the control of its master – not a floppy marshmallow. Pliable strength. It follows, therefore, that people pliant in the purposes of God shall inherit the earth. How does all this relate to a method of praying?

## Prayerful submission to the mission

What we are targeting in this chapter is a coalition of meekness and a life of prayer. As we pray to the LORD with humility and live out our prayer in a gentle spirit, we shall see our inheritance materialise. In exchange for our abstract prayer for the earth we want to see concrete results.

In actual fact, we are furthering the *mission* of God and that *mission* looks like something substantial. We want to see the *mission* expand and that looks like something concrete: that all nations will know the just reign of God, that every single person will come to a saving knowledge of Jesus Christ, that the planet's resources are rightly stewarded, that diseases will be healed, Covid-19 arrested and wars cease. As night follows day, it is inevitable that Christ's *mission* to the earth will advance as our prayer and action line up with the will of God.

And because this kingdom stuff is such a huge agenda it follows that our commitment should mirror the surrender of Jesus Christ to the plan of his Father. Even though the whole earth belongs to the LORD, Christians have a directive to be co-workers with Christ. We are to pray that the Lᴏʀᴅ's kingdom, for which Christ died, truly comes with power and that his will be done in all spheres of society.

When we become answers to our own humble prayer and step into arenas of influence with humility, we become agents of change and the mission progresses. As a bonus we get to share in the inheritance. How cool is that? So let us get praying with heartfelt conviction and renewed energy!

## Jesus

Jesus' subservience led him to crucifixion. But that death and resurrection won salvation for all the peoples of the earth. The result of his obedience to death was the salvation of the entire planet – in theory. It is up to each one to actualise the personal salvation won for us and choose eternal life. Jesus' inheritance was the earth. Working with him to bring in the harvest is the prayerful task before us.

## Benefits

I hear you say that this is all very well but so far everything is extremely theoretical and somewhat airy-fairy. *How do we maximise humility?*

*How do we measure it? How do we know whether we are being meek and mild or simply lazy and avoiding the issues?* Here is one practical example from my own experience (and there are countless others) of how this exercise works.

At one point in my life, fully committed to the idea that a particular work situation was a call from God to advance the mission, I faced nonetheless insurmountable problems – humanly speaking. It felt as though ineffectual administration was set to ruin and ravage every aspect of the role, so that a rocking boat in a storm was better suited for survival than my lone beacon in a sea of mismanagement. I persevered, I plugged away, and I prayed. At first I prayed, rather arrogantly: 'God remove me for I am worth more than these troubles.' Then I saw the results of my labours as lives were transformed, learning progressed exponentially and opportunities for preaching fell into my lap. Then I gave in, submitted, and began to pray: 'Despite the ridiculousness and inconvenience, continue to use me to further your kingdom here.' And God did and more territory was won.

Then one day, after an especially horrendous incident, I caught a glimpse of our enemy's tactics to annihilate the opposition, me. Something rose up in me and I went to war in prayer to contest the ground. I simply refused to give in to the powers of darkness trying to undermine my witness to Christ. Inwardly my surrender was to Jesus; outwardly and towards others I moved under his restraint and control until little by little the problems abated and there was peace on all sides.

## Who will go with me?

When it comes to spiritual direction in prayer, we are faced with a multitude of options, methods and exercises. This Workout is not intended to provide a path for any one of these. The reader must decide how best to proceed. What the Workout in prayer has advised is that the best method to build up one's prayer life is to see every prayer as an act of submission to the mission of God. However personal our prayer, we are ultimately in the service of our Master and the way we change is the way he will win others for eternity.

Therefore, the very best guide to prayer is to keep praying 'Come Holy Spirit'. To lean on the Spirit, to pray in the Spirit, to tap in to the resources of the Spirit is to learn the divine currents. We pray a prayer of fire for the illumination of the mind, for the Spirit of God to break down barriers in our head, to permeate and penetrate our thinking so that we pray with fresh insight. We pray that the Holy Spirit brings to us the things of Jesus, softens our hearts with his compassion and makes us tender to the plight of the poor. We pray that the Spirit strengthens our will to do the divine will without faltering. We invite the Spirit to keep us strong in body, to be unflinching in our devotion to Christ, to keep at it. And if we are brave, we might ask the Holy Spirit to give us new tongues with which to pray and intercede:

> *In the same way, the Spirit helps us in our weakness. We do not know what we ought to pray for, but the Spirit himself intercedes for us through wordless groans. And he who searches our hearts knows the mind of the Spirit, because the Spirit intercedes for God's people in accordance with the will of God.*
> (ROM. 8:26–27)

You may invite a spiritual director to walk with you in your journey to share helpful nuggets for prayer and to keep tabs on your prayer life for a season, to give you check-up appointments if you like. Or you may choose to pray with one or two others, to practise praying together out loud and often. All these customs are available to us. The main thing is not to stop praying – not ever!

## Working out in prayer

To work is to pray, so goes the old adage. The Greek boy in the gymnasium worked hard at wrestling–one of the sports earning the most celebrity status. Prayer is like a wrestling match with an adversary. There is Jacob battling it out at the River Jabbok with the Almighty (Gen. 32:22–32). We find Jesus up against it in the wilderness, his opponent Satan himself (Luke 4:1–13). Then there are the disciples in Gethsemane, straining against frail human nature, asleep on their prayer watch like every disciple down the ages (Luke 22:45–46). In exercising prayer, we need all the help we can get. We need the help of the Holy Spirit.

### ▷ Step one

First we recognise that we can change the way we pray in order to excel even in our weakness. For example, although prayer is often in our heads (especially here in the West), more often than not in the Bible it is a muscular, physical activity: speaking out loud, kneeling or prostrating on the ground, lifting up arms and hands in thanksgiving or petition, walking about or climbing a hill, speaking out loud in the Holy Spirit in new tongues.

There are biblical precedents for all these gestures and postures in the praying of disciples, prophets, priests and kings. In some way, the anatomy can demonstrate piety. The sinner beating his breast at the back of the synagogue is commended by Jesus. Bartimaeus crying out for mercy with great embarrassing shouts is heard by Jesus and healed. Whatever we find works best for ourselves, that we should do, for surely our aim in working out in prayer is to become better at it!

## Step two

Choose a place to pray and go there every day out of sheer unadulterated habit, like brushing your teeth. Never give up on this even when you do not feel like it. You brush your teeth anyway, even when you would rather not, otherwise others will notice. (Bad breath!) When we neglect to pray for a day, then two or three days, we notice the difference and others will experience our lack of prayer, too. (No divine breath!)

### Step three

For the purpose of developing spiritual muscle, choose an awkward, uncomfortable scenario. Begin to pray using the LORD's Prayer and the words: Your kingdom come, your will be done, on earth as it is in heaven. Pray in faith, pray until you see the shift, pray for breakthrough.

# WORKOUT FOUR

## Hunger for righteousness and the fast

Our world is full of food – and famine. Celebrity chefs and pick of the week recipes jostle with hungry migrants and famished children on our screens. *Well, there's nothing I can do about it, it's the government's problem – unless it happens to me and I have to find a food bank. The gnawing ache of an empty stomach and weakened resilience – may it not be so in my lifetime in the lives of those close to me. I will fight tooth and nail for food for my family, for myself.*

The drive to avoid hunger at any cost is contested by the latest thing: the fast. Up-to-date thinkers and neuroscientists stress its benefits for a healthy mind and body: the 15-hour fast, skipping a meal, one day a week, two weeks a year, and so on. Actually, these ideas are passé as they simply tap into the customs of Ancient China, Siberia or the Celts, for example, where fasting was undertaken for therapeutic or spiritual, intellectual or political reasons. Peoples of all the world religions fast, and Jews and Christians have done so for millennia.

Returning to our theme of strengthening our core, we note with interest that in Ancient Greece fasting was a means to prepare athletes' bodies for physical training ahead of the Olympic Games. That's good then, we're on the right track! I have to say that in my experience the business of fasting and spiritual effort are inextricably linked. Going without food, or even a reduced diet does seem to focus the mind and the spirit, and although physical strength can be sapped, somehow there is more energy overall. If that is the case, how then shall we proceed?

## Fourth beatitude

There is no better way to remind ourselves of spiritual priorities when it comes to appetite than the fourth beatitude: 'Blessed are those who hunger and thirst for righteousness, for they will be filled' (Matt. 5:6). In this saying, the LORD is accentuating a bumper infilling of the soul with the food of righteousness. The fullness of the soul is guaranteed when there is a desire or craving for righteousness. *Yes, that's all very well, but it's this word 'righteousness', which is confusing. What does it mean and how do we define it as it sounds a very 'religious' word?*

The word 'righteousness' translates the Hebrew word *sedeq* in the Old Testament. In the Septuagint (LXX), which is the Greek translation of the Old Testament, and in the New Testament, the word *dikaiosunē* is used. The words in both languages describe both the morally *right character* of God and also his *right behaviour*. To be righteous, therefore, is to *be* completely right like God and to *act* like God. We are told that there are only three righteous men in the Old Testament: Daniel, Job and Noah (Ezek. 14:14). In the New Testament we learn that only God is righteous (Rom. 3:10–11). We also discover that only Jesus can rescue us from sin and make us righteous through his death and resurrection (Rom. 3:21–26). We cannot make ourselves righteous, try as we might, for it is the Holy Spirit who works his power in us to give us a right character and to produce in us right actions (Rom. 8:10–11).

*Phew, that lets us off the hook. It seems that righteousness (being right with God) and the fruits of righteousness (deeds and attitudes) are God's work in us.* Right! *Well then, surely that defeats the whole idea of exercising a discipline to 'improve' my righteousness. And that is a good point, but hold on, how about if*

*I begin to fast a little to see whether God has more opportunity, more leeway in my life to change me and to reshape my character to become more like him?* So, we are going to consider making a little more room in our lives for our relationship with the LORD Jesus to grow, in fact to speed up, which means creating a hunger for more of him. And if that means doing away with food, in some form or another, and replacing physical sustenance with spiritual nourishment, bring it on!

## The Christian fast

The early Christians modelled their fasting on the Jewish custom of two days a week. Since then different parts of Christendom have alternative ways of fasting: the Lenten fast, the 40 days of giving up something nice to eat or drink as a token sacrifice; lean days (going without meat or fish); days of abstinence, of abstaining from certain food or drink. And so on. Up to extreme forms of extended periods of denial.

According to the age-old Christian teaching, a pure fast is unto the LORD and for him. During a fast we make time for God by praying, listening and reading Scripture or a devotional book. Although we may be at work or shopping or child-minding or engaged in a variety of activities at the same time, our focus is the LORD. As we push away our hungers and approach him with humility and in weakness, his power reaches us.

*May we set before God a personal agenda?* For instance, fasting for justice in a work situation. Or fasting for a friend who is seriously ill. Perhaps fasting for the future, for breakthrough and change. These personal life circumstances are common to us all. There is no harm in our meaning business with God and, as it were, trying to get his attention through fasting. However, our aim in the exercise is not to solve the pressing problem but to meet with the LORD. As we do so, the pressures we give to him and any answered prayer or resolutions are by-products of that obedience.

*Is there evidence for political protest fasts?* Indeed there is, but probably better to call these exercises solidarity hunger strikes. I was deeply impacted at meeting Bernard Wrankmore once over dinner at my parents' home. In 1971, this radical Mission to Seamen priest had gone without food for 67 days on Signal Hill in Cape Town to protest the death, in detention, of a Muslim cleric. Although the inquest he demanded was never held, his hunger strike brought home the reality of police brutality under the Apartheid regime.

Several years later, I was one of many student hunger strikers, who for eight days protested the death, in detention, of a Black Consciousness leader. I cannot say that all this brought me any closer to Jesus Christ; I suppose I was more concerned in partnering with a revolt to apply moral pressure to an unjust system. Going without food sensitised me to the oppressed and I may have grown in compassion, although it was the cause rather than mercy that drove my actions.

## Jesus

Jesus fasted. As a Jew, he fasted as was the Jewish custom. He fasted in the desert in preparation for his mission. He took it for granted that his followers would fast. How this was to be done was ultra-important: not with gloomy forbearance but with joy and in secret without fanfare. Fasting for God.

## Benefits

My own testimony will have to suffice here, as I cannot speak for anyone else. In a life of fasting – from one day, to three days, to ten-day liquid fasts, to 40 days (fruit at night) – I have found the LORD to be present and active and doing stuff in me that I could not do myself. I have also had to contend with my enemy, the devil, and my own passions and desires. I have discovered that fasting can be unpleasant and not easy. At times it is exhilarating and effortless. The benefits are extraordinary: growth in Christ, conquering old sins, love for others, advancing the mission.

## Who will go with me?

Probably no one! I have not found fasting a popular topic of conversation in Christian circles and, if it does come up, it is often accompanied by mutterings: my health, my temperament, my lifestyle, my work and family commitments. I couldn't possibly! If I am looking for a friend to accompany me on a fast I will probably seek in vain, unless a group of friends decide to fast for a dire situation in one of their lives. Or intercessors fast for the country before an election, or for a social justice issue, or for healing for a work mate or colleague or relative.

*Do we give up on an ancient discipline because we find ourselves in the minority?* Absolutely not! This is precisely when we need to excel. Find a friend to back you in prayer as you fast; who knows, they may end up fasting with you. If you are really serious about this exercise, seek out a spiritual director who understands the fast, such as a monk or a nun, and ask for counsel and wisdom in your fast. As you push through the barriers you will discover a deep-seated and energising joy.

## Working out in fasting

These are simply suggestions and, as with physical exercise, each person has to go at their own pace. You may be content to stick at the first step; you may desire to go on, but it is all up to you. If you think it wise, you might consider consulting a GP about an extended fast.

### Step one

Start small. There is no point in having a high ideal of 40 days when you've never skipped a meal. Try missing a meal and using that hour to pray or read Scripture. Then progress to fasting two meals and eating in the evening. Try that once a week. Try going without caffeine and having juices or water only during the day as you fast.

### Step two

Develop a personal routine of missing a meal or choosing a day to fast and do this every week until it becomes a habit. Monitor how your relationship with Jesus is going as you exercise this discipline.

### ▶ Step three

Branch out to longer periods of fasting as you are led by the LORD. For example, you might try two days of going without food and drinking fruit juices or water only. You can extend this time as you feel led by God and with the counsel of someone wiser who has experience of fasting. Some fast for 10 days or 21 days or even 40 days. There are no rules but divine wisdom and help from others is always advisable to avoid unnecessary trouble.

# WORKOUT FIVE

## Mercy and anointing oil

Oil was commonplace in the exercise schedule of an Ancient Greek athlete. The underlying sense in all the theories advanced for this practice is that anointing the body with oil was a healthy thing to do. Perhaps oil warmed and limbered up the muscles before exercise and the glowing skin of the athlete was aesthetically pleasing and offered protection from the elements during exercise, or that the oil was a symbol of sacrifice, of a body given for the glory of the gods. What we do know is that each athlete carried his own oil in a small flask for application when all dirt had been scraped away after his exertions. Clearly it was thought that the properties in oil pampered, cleansed and healed.

In natural cures today, we recognise the balm of oil, the soothing touch of bath oil, of lotions for tired or dry skin, or feet or hands, and the oily strength of the masseur's pressure on bodily aches and pains. We can easily transpose these ideas to our spiritual workout plan when it comes to the age-old Christian convention of anointing with oil. On a spiritual level, the oil represents the work of the Holy Spirit in bringing the presence of Jesus Christ to the one needing a healing, forgiving touch. The oil is a visible and outward sign of an inward grace from the LORD. Having said that, let us attempt to bring together the art of oil anointing and the fifth beatitude as we continue our Workout.

## Fifth beatitude

Jesus announced to his disciples: 'Blessed are the merciful, for they will be shown mercy' (Matt. 5:7). It would be rather tempting to try to find a common derivative root in the Greek words, 'mercy' (*eleos*) and 'oil' or 'olive oil' (*elaion*). Unfortunately we cannot do that with integrity; but we can possibly *feel* a similarity between these two concepts as they *sound* quite similar. As we have seen, oil or olive oil (*elaion*) was the anointing oil used after a bathe or before a wrestling match or exercise at the gymnasium and sometimes it was rose-scented or simply scented oil, *muron*, our English 'myrrh'. In this beatitude, the word for mercy, pity or compassion is *eleos*. Those with a liturgical background will recognise the *Kyrie eleison* prayer: LORD, have mercy.

An example of these two words coming together is in Jesus' parable of what is means to be a good neighbour (Luke 10:30–37). The Samaritan tended the man who fell among brigands by pouring 'oil' [*elaion*] on his wounds (v34). The definition of the good neighbour is 'the one who had mercy [*eleos*] on him' (v37), the one who poured out upon the stranger a healing oil, a balm of mercy.

But what exactly is mercy? Recently, I had the pleasure of meeting a charming little girl called Mercy. What a good name! Her English parents showed good neighbourliness in Africa and dedicated quite a few years of their lives to charitable building work projects. This couple demonstrated that the spiritual discipline of showing mercy is part and parcel of their surrender to God. Working out by exercising mercy can never be self-centred; it is always outgoing towards another, altruistic and without selfish motives.

One of the loveliest descriptions of the quality of mercy is Portia's speech in *The Merchant of Venice*. In fact, the English actress and television producer, Joanna Lumley, quoted these exact lines recently, with regard to Cyrus II of Persia (died 530 BC), who was so powerful but treated his subjects and captured nations with mercy, an attribute she declared we needed more of today in our leaders. The first four lines of the speech are a comment on the fifth beatitude. The quality of mercy is 'twice blest' as both the receiver and the giver are its beneficiaries. As we ask for, and receive, God's mercy, may we show mercy to others:

> *The quality of mercy is not strained.*
> *It droppeth as the gentle rain from heaven*
> *Upon the place beneath. It is twice blest:*
> *It blesseth him that gives and him that takes.*
> *…*
> *It is an attribute to God Himself;*
> *We do pray for mercy,*
> *And that same prayer doth teach us all to render*
> *The deeds of mercy.*
>
> (WILLIAM SHAKESPEARE, THE MERCHANT OF VENICE, ACT 4, SCENE 1)

## Anointing oil

So what does the Church believe about anointing oil and how can this practice be seen as a spiritual discipline? There are three ways in which the

New Testament shows that anointing with oil is a regular routine. First, the disciples anoint the sick with oil (Mark 6:13) and the Early Church clearly teaches that oil and healing prayer is available for those who are ill (James 5:14). Second, the notion of forgiveness of sins is underlined in this healing habit (James 5:16). Third, Jesus briefs his followers about fasting, that they are to put oil on their heads as a sign to themselves of doing something good for God, although others will be unaware (Matt. 6:17).

On the first point, the ancient practice of anointing the sick is adhered to by almost every denomination from Anglo-Catholic to Pentecostal, probably because the scriptural precedent is crystal clear. Although every Greek athlete had his own vial of oil, this is not always the case in Christendom, where the athletes for Christ have to be elders, priests or recognised ministers before they may anoint. Fluidity exists in Nonconformist or freer streams where all may anoint and many do indeed carry their own small flasks, at the ready for any request for healing. Perhaps the brandy barrel around the neck of the great St Bernard – that extraordinary mountain rescue dog – illustrates the point.

On the second point, to be a carrier of

healing oil is a serious business, particularly as it pertains to the sacrament of penance, upheld by a large part of the Church. Not one of us is a good judge in our own case and at times we need the discernment of another. Here ordination is required. The penitent comes before the servant of God and in prayer delivers himself or herself of the burden of sin and guilt. Forgiveness and pardon are given and received and the whole process might be accompanied by anointing oil as a seal of divine grace and assurance.

However, even without a licence we are told as members of the Church to 'confess your sins to each other and pray for each other so that you may be healed' (James 5:16). This does not always sit well with a privatised religion, a piety limited to the self, me and Jesus, me and the Holy Spirit. But the injunction for transparency between Christians is well-timed in our image-conscious era. Instead of obsessing over our appearance, clothing, fantastic lifestyles and enviable photographs on social media platforms, let us pause and think about showing close friends our not-so-nice bits. Such open friendship can be marvellously healing and therapeutic. Accountability relationships are a most necessary way of keeping accounts of our sins and failings, not only with God, but also with one another. In short, bring back confession, the old habit of penance.

On the third point, that of fasting and oil, we are less informed than the Jews. Probably our contemporary equivalent is to anoint not the head, but the entrance to our homes, the front door and every outside entry point, as a reminder that Christ is the head of this house and all its occupants and drives away every evil influence.

## Jesus

We are not told that Jesus used oil for healing. What we are told is that he himself was anointed in preparation for his death and burial (see John 12:1–8). Like an athlete preparing for strenuous exertion, Jesus of Nazareth had his own masseuse. A woman took a jar of expensive nard and anointed Jesus in preparation for his own physical and mental exertions, his cross and torturous death. Jesus is the wounded healer and from him flows all the anointing for health, healing and forgiveness we could ever seek.

## Benefits

Whatever our practice, the power of Christ is ready to heal. This I discovered when, beset by wracking chronic back pain a week after hitting a wall in a dangerous sledge accident, I approached a total stranger, a robed clergyman, at the end of a weekday morning eucharist and requested anointing for healing. Without batting an eyelid he disappeared into his vestry, reappearing with the oil. I knelt at the altar rail and he prayed a brief prayer, never once asking what I wanted or which part of my anatomy, soul or spirit was quite so desperate. I got up and left. The following day I came off all pain killers and to this day have had no effects of that accident.

Being a shy person, I find confession out loud quite hard but I do try with select friends every so often. Once, as a young adult, I found myself admitting to a healing group that I was very full of anger and torrid stuff and felt so guilty. As they laid hands on me and prayed, I became aware that every single person on earth is in the same boat and that we are born in sin (Psa. 51:5). As that realisation hit me I was filled with joy and thanksgiving that I shared a nature in common with all and was not a lost cause.

## Who will go with me?

There is no easy answer to this question in the matter of oil anointing for healing or confession of sin as there are chasms separating the denominations. In the Anglo-Catholic stream and from personal experience, I have no doubt at all that there is merit in kneeling or sitting with a priest and confessing a besetting sin or listing a catalogue of sins and receiving absolution and anointing with oil. I have found this to be a tremendously therapeutic practice. Why? I cannot say, except that the grace of God was present and I was relieved in a way I could not have been on my own.

On a guided retreat, it may be the retreat conductor's way to hear a confession and this has certainly been my experience. People have found their way to an interview with me and it has been a time of unburdening, a moment when they have offloaded their sins in an informal manner and I have been there to hear them and then promptly to forget them as they went straight to the cross of Christ. Often this half hour has been a time of healing and cleansing prayer of the mind or emotions and it is here that the oil of anointing finds a place.

On the whole, the Nonconformist and Pentecostal practice is to rely on elders to anoint and for each penitent to go to the Lord on their own. However, in prayer partners or prayer triplets when honesty prevails, there can be a confiding and intimate confession of sins to one another.

All these practices are healing. Our prayer ought to be to the Holy Spirit of truth to convict us of sin (John 16:8–9) and who indeed does this work at times without our consent. We squirm and are made uncomfortable as he draws near to bring our shortcomings to light.

## Working out with mercy and oil

How do we become more merciful? In my experience some people are just better at this than I will ever be. But I do find that when I do not have the words or even an appropriate feeling, then the oil does the trick. There is something about its symbolic nature that inspires contact with God when I am not up to the task.

### Step one

Be at peace with the thought that the oil is a symbol, not the thing itself, of the healing properties that are in Jesus and at our disposal by virtue of the cross and resurrection. Healing is in him and we turn to him and not the oil. But use the oil yourself in healing prayer, if this is the practice in your church and you are in good standing and right relationship. If not, then call on the elders and vicar to pray for friends and family and to anoint with oil. Let us begin to resurrect this practice because the resurrection of Jesus sets us free to pray for healing and we need all the help we can get in our sceptical secular society.

## Step two

Be mindful of the value of accountability relationships and check out your friends at church or in your group to see who might fit the bill when it comes to confessing sins to one another from time to time. But be aware that this should never become a forced or legalistic action. We cannot make ourselves holy; we can only open a door for the Spirit to act upon us.

## Step three

Try consecrating or re-consecrating your home to Christ by anointing its doors and external portals with oil. Drive away all evil forces and seat Christ on the throne of your home.

# WORKOUT SIX

## Purity and pilgrimage

Did you notice during the period of extreme COVID-19 lockdown measures how we became a walking nation overnight? Everyone was out walking, young, elderly, the very old, the very young, babies in prams and men and women who had never walked, walked. And walked. The world walked for exercise and to get out, joining thronging multitudes in bygone times who walked everywhere in daily life, not for exercise but as the only way of getting about.

People of the major world religions walk, going on pilgrimage to visit shrines or holy sites or places of significance. And Christians, too, have pilgrimage at the heart of their faith. You may have heard of that extremely long pilgrims' way, the Camino de Santiago, a network of paths leading to the shrine of the apostle Saint James the Great in the cathedral of Santiago de Compostela in north-western Spain. You may know someone who has done this walk, or part of this walk and encountered other people *in via*, on the way, who helped them or pointed the way. In the New Testament Christians were known as people of 'The Way', pilgrims en route to heaven, following Jesus who called himself the way. A physical journey to a specific destination can be a spiritual representation of that greater heavenly pilgrimage upon which all Christians are embarked.

Pilgrimage for spiritual reasons does not have to be a specially organised programme with a group, although fellow travellers can be a real bonus. (Recall some of the entertaining accounts of the pilgrims in Chaucer's *Canterbury Tales*.) Indeed, a casual walk on one's own can turn into a spiritual experience, as I discovered one sunny early morning during the national lockdown. As I walked along the Pewsey Vale, I came across, quite by accident, the ancient Wansdyke trail. It was no big deal but I immediately felt like a Christian pilgrim on a primal path, turning to prayer, seeking the LORD, feeling united to him on that glorious spring morning. As I tuned in, I felt connected to the source of life itself: *pulsating* life all around, the little hills, the little lambs, the little orchids and buttercups – God in it all and all in all, the Creator God who made it all. What could I do but worship and praise and attune my heart to him?

Going back in time hundreds of years ago, we know that the fabulous ancient routes of medieval pilgrimage to Jerusalem were marked by abbeys offering hospitality and prayer to the intrepid pilgrims. And people today are seeking that kind of break in life's journey, so it was with delight that my eye fell upon an article in the *Financial Times*. The writer, a journalist of 30 years and in search of a radical humility, journeyed on a sort of pilgrimage to a monastery where all community life was conducted in silence, and, much to her astonishment, in a *companionable* silence. Having explored the benefits of silence in a previous chapter, let's link the concept of pilgrimage with the sixth beatitude.

## Sixth beatitude

At the heart of the sixth beatitude is innocence, incorruptibility, blamelessness. These wonderful virtues become the doorstep into heavenly vision. We stand on the threshold, on tiptoe straining to catch a glimpse of that other world. In this beatitude we are assured that 'Blessed are the pure in heart, for they will see God' (Matt.

5:8). Thus we realise that purity is the link between the pilgrim and the beatific vision – that rapturous delight in God for himself. But what does it mean and how shall we grasp and attain such an ethereal aspect?

First, we must unpack the word 'purity' linguistically before moving on to pilgrimage as a means to the end, which is the vision of God. Think of 'pure air'. In the sixth beatitude the Greek adjective used for 'pure' gives us a clue. It is *katharos* meaning clean, pure or clear. Our English derivative, 'catharsis', is the process of cleansing release and relief from suppressed emotions and feelings. We might say, for example, 'Seeing Toby that day and unburdening myself to him was a cathartic experience.' *Katharos* has a raft of associations, which include ethical, physical and ritual cleansing. For the Jew *katharos* meant purging and purifying through right sacrifices and offerings of lambs and goats.

During temple worship, Isaiah the prophet-priest has an overwhelming experience of heaven opened to him and cries out, 'I saw the Lord, high and exalted, seated on a throne', but is then completely overcome by his own impurity, 'Woe to me… I am ruined! For I am a man of unclean lips, and I live among a people of unclean lips, and

my eyes have seen the King, the LORD Almighty.'
In response, a flying seraph descends with a
burning coal to press against those unclean
lips and refine by fire (see Isa. 6:1–7). Evidently,
purity of heart brings its reward of seeing God, *or*
the other way around, of seeing one's sinfulness
in the light of God's holiness.

One day, when we meet face to face with the
LORD, we shall be changed in the twinkling of an
eye, but at present we are in Christ's crucible. And
this state of in-betweenness, imperfection and
perfection, is probably the reason we do not see
the LORD plainly. And yet we long to be one of the
enlightened ones who do see beyond the everyday,
beyond the current climate, the prevailing crisis,
the problem, the sense of loss or of pain. We
struggle for God's vision yet yearn for resolution
of life's troubles, for an ending to the drama, for a
place of peaceful bliss. For blessedness.

The sixth beatitude tells us that we are blessed,
full of abundant and exuberant happiness when
we are pure in heart. When we are cleansed
and resolved and our hearts are set on the LORD
in a single-minded and steadfast devotion and
preoccupation with the stuff of eternity. But how
shall we achieve this state?

## Pilgrimage and purity

Christians are not among those who have made themselves pure by some kind of cathartic self-cleansing. Instead, their hearts are purified by the blood of Jesus Christ's sacrifice on the cross. And this is not a one-off event (although initial repentance and turning to Christ surely is), but an ongoing journey of being made holy. Unlike many other world religions with their rituals of purification, a Christian is never dependent on the outward actions. Yet probably most of us need an outward action to try to express an inner resolve. To decide for purity is, in itself, a decisive moment. To decide to make a journey to become more pure is a pipedream, or is it? The psalmist writes: 'Blessed are those whose strength is in you, whose hearts are set on pilgrimage. As they pass through the Valley of Baka, they make it a place of springs' (Psa. 84:5–6). The promise in the psalm is that motivated journeying is not a wearying and gloomy affair, but, quite to the contrary, a strength-filled exercise leading to oases. And these life-giving springs are, of course, to be interpreted in a spiritual sense.

Perhaps you have already thought that the very *idea* of pilgrimage in a pandemic-locked world is ludicrous! (Here's hoping things have improved since writing this.) However, we are not imprisoned irrevocably. There are ways out and around and through dilemmas of travel to circumnavigate our apathy that there is nothing we can do. There is absolutely *something* we can do to make pilgrimage happen. The persecuted Chinese Christians literally *ran* to neighbouring villages to join fellow worshippers. And we know the phenomenal rate of growth of the church in that Communist-locked land.

There is something about getting perspective as a disciple of Jesus, which time out in a disciplined giving of our time to the LORD can bring. Watch a buzzard or red kite catch the currents, see those mighty birds of prey settle on the wind, soar, swoop and pounce in such a matter-of-fact manner, height giving total accuracy and speed and success to their project. So it is with the wind of the Holy Spirit. Go to where the Spirit blows and feel the difference. Sometimes this means going somewhere else, away from a comfortable living space to a place of dislocation, a geographical relocation, a journey to pinpoint the exact state of the soul. A pilgrimage.

## Jesus

Jesus walked – everywhere. And the crowds followed in his dust. I imagine at times they ran to keep up with him, this fit and energetic man of the road, of the mountains and hills. Many of his signs and wonders were miracles done on the road while walking. Before dawn, Jesus rose from sleep and, leaving his domicile, walked and prayed.

## Benefits

Two significant moments come to mind when I consider pilgrimage. Seated on a rock overlooking the Jezreel Valley in Israel while my fellow pilgrims went in to a church, I became aware of a vision of myself walking on a road to a church building, which then disappeared and was replaced by an impression of Jesus. I knew what God was saying: Seek the Lord and not the Church.

Joining the hustle and bustle of pilgrims in Assisi and following in the footsteps of the twelfth-century holy man, Francis, I left the crowds to find the woods where he had walked and conversed with his Lord. As I did so, I was transported into a clean and open spiritual space of unutterable peace.

## Who will go with me?

The very best companion on our pilgrimage is the LORD himself. Recall the famous Emmaus road on the day of the resurrection when the risen LORD joins the two friends as they walk and talk about the tumultuous events of that weekend (Luke 24:13–35). Their burning hearts as Jesus breaks bread testifies to this powerful encounter. Is it enough to simply recollect, to imagine how it must have been? It is not enough. We, too, need a burning heart, an experience of Jesus as we pilgrimage. We need the presence of the Holy Spirit to bring to us the things of Jesus. Jesus said: 'All that belongs to the Father is mine. That is why I said the Spirit will receive from me what he will make known to you' (John 16:15).

And so we pray again: Come Holy Spirit and bring to me what is in Jesus. Make me like Jesus. Do your work in me and change me into his likeness as I journey. Sometimes the Spirit comes as warmth, as heat, as a whisper, as a loud voice, as an impression, as wind, as a picture or image. His purpose is to draw us, not to himself, but to Jesus. He walks alongside us: *paraklētos*, the one called alongside, our Advocate and Defender.

However, because we are very human, we need friends on the way and that means physical fellow pilgrims. We may have a regular group with whom we make pilgrimage annually to the island of Iona or Holy Island, for example. Not simply bird watchers (although that might come into it) but people who worship and pray together as they travel and abide in these ancient sites of Christian life. Or we may decide to travel to a house for a guided retreat with a spiritual director. We may do this on a regular basis, two or three times a year, the consultations with a trusted leader being refreshing oases.

## Working out in pilgrimage

As with the ancient Greeks, so with the 'latest' neuroscientific thinking: physical exercise is not only good for us, it is the very best way of aging well. And the more we dedicate to God our working out by walking regime, the more we shall hear and see him and learn his ways and progress in prayer. Little by little, step by step, pilgrims on the way. The physical exercise of putting one foot in front of another to go a certain distance, however long or short, has to start somewhere with a mind made up to try it out.

▷ **Step one**
Build pilgrimage into your everyday life by using

the walking you already do as a meditation on spiritual matters. For instance, take ten minutes on your walk to work from the train or bus station or car park to fix your mind on Jesus rather than on the coffee you will buy. Ask him to speak to you as you walk. Use part of your lunch hour to walk and pray. Or, having packed the shopping in the car, choose to stroll somewhere for a few minutes to think more spiritually than usual. Or walk out into your garden or patio or field or street, choosing to think on the LORD and to pray. Walk and talk with the Saviour! Use your step-tracker to factor in steps and get mileage out of spiritual endeavour!

### Step two

Branch out and go for a longer walk in your city, village or countryside. Plan it. Go with a partner or friend or group or entirely alone. Plot a route and ask God to refine your walking and to make it a spiritual adventure. Seek him in the creation, in the faces of others, in the sounds and senses you feel en route. In other words, bring the LORD into the physical exercise. You may be surprised at the outcome, at what you see and hear.

## ▷ Step three

Go to a place, a hermitage, a retreat house, a bothy in the mountains, an island, travelling by train or car or plane or boat. Getting there is part of the pilgrimage, integral to the journey away, away from the comfort zone, from family and friends, to seek the LORD. For the wild at heart this is the pinnacle, the ideal.

# WORKOUT SEVEN

## Peacemakers and offerings

In the sanctuary of Olympia in Ancient Greece a flame, ignited only by the rays of the sun, burned perpetually. Outside, fires from this permanent flame burned on altars for animal sacrifices to the gods. Fire was of divine origin and a sacred element. A Greek athlete would bring a torch of pure fire to the altar as a sign of his worship. Today, some months before the Olympic Games begin, the torch, ignited only by the rays of the sun from the ruins of the temple in Olympia, is transported to that ancient stadium and given to the first runner. So begins the next cycle of sporting prowess.

Pure fire is a symbol of divinity and testimony to the bowed down worshipper. Ancient Greeks were serious about their gods and their physical feats and achievements were their paeans of praise. We shall use this imagery to illuminate the spiritual discipline of service, the dedication of one's gifts – of money or of charitable deeds – to God and to our neighbour. And we shall see that, just like the Ancient Greek athlete, Christian almsgiving (a quaint, old-fashioned word for gifts of money) and sacrifice are acts of pure worship, of pure fire if you like.

What does the New Testament say about all this? Well, I am exhorted to honour God by the offering of my body 'as a living sacrifice, holy and pleasing to God' because this oblation of myself is my 'true and proper worship' (Rom. 12:1). The Greek word used in this passage for worship is *leitourgia*, which means 'work of the people' along the lines of the act of public worship or liturgy. But to think that times at gathered places (church, home groups, prayer meetings) as the *only* way to serve fails to draw out the deeper meaning in the text. The whole of one's inferior, creaturely existence, body and soul, is to be consecrated to the superior, to the Creator. The whole life as a whole offering. However, we cannot draw a line here and say, that's it, I am wholly sold out to God – inwardly. We must demonstrate our worship in word and deed – outwardly.

Jesus is quite clear that what we do for our neighbour is part and parcel of the gift: 'Therefore, if you are offering your gift at the altar and there remember that your brother or sister has something against you, leave your gift there in front of the altar. First go and be reconciled to them; then come and offer your gift' (Matt. 5:23–24).

In other words, let your fire be transparently pure! It's no good at all behaving piously at the collection plate with money, cheques or tithes, while inwardly seething and at odds with a fellow believer. Be at peace with God and with one another is the nub of the matter. And where better to place our quest for peace than at the seventh beatitude, to which we now turn in this Workout.

## Seventh beatitude

'Blessed are the peacemakers, for they will be called children of God' (Matt. 5:9). *Why are these people who make peace more especially called 'children [or sons] of God'? Surely anyone who confesses Jesus Christ as Lord is a child of God? Can I still be called a child of God if I am at war with another person? And, more importantly for our purposes, how does being a peacemaker tie in with the idea of gifts and offerings?*

The short answer to the question of sonship is bound to the concept of inheritance. To be overabundantly blessed and bouncing around full of the joys is in the largesse of the Father's goodness to those who practise peace. In other words, peacemakers are more likely to be joy bringers and happiness holders than gloomy and discontented disciples going about griping and at odds with everybody. A down-on-the-world, miserable follower of Jesus is still his child, but the one who lives in the fullness of blessedness in that sonship is the one who lives in all the inheritance of the cross.

On the cross, God was in Christ reconciling the whole world to himself and making us the ministers of reconciliation (see 2 Cor. 5:19). Those who adhere to the teaching of Jesus Christ, therefore, who keep short accounts with others, do not let the sun go down on their anger and choose to make peace, will be living in the blessed benefits of the cross. They will be filled with an extravagant joy, says this beatitude. *How then does being an ambassador of peace fit in with being a devoted giver to God of tithes and offerings, and services to others?*

## The discipline of gifts and service

My peace with God was won by the finished work of Jesus Christ on the cross and without my help. We're all in the same boat and the ground is level at the cross. Therefore, my deeds of devoted service ought to be tempered with a measure of humility, knowing that there but for the grace of God go I, that the LORD looks on my heart and not at the magnitude of my gift or service.

Do you recall how Jesus commends the poor widow who put in a tiny offering, which he said was her entire life? In contrast, he exposes the pompous givers who cannot give alms without broadcasting it very loudly on the street. In actual fact it was customary for a trumpeter to go before these overenthusiastic benefactors, and the minute the offering was placed the whole synagogue knew about it: it's called blowing your own trumpet.

Jesus calls these people 'hypocrites', which the Greek word *hupokritēs* has to a tee, in other words, one who pretends to be what one is not. The word *hypokritikos* goes one step further and is used metaphorically in classical Greek of one playing a part on the stage. In Greek tragedy, these actors wore masks for their roles. Thus the LORD is playing on words here, rather humorously it has to be said, to point a finger at these mask-wearing pretenders. Off with the masks and on with proper humble giving! The rest is humbug!

*Yes, but how does pretending to be a cheerful giver*

*when one is really concerned with reward help us in our view of peacemaker?* In that giving money to the tune of a fanfare or doing works of charity in order to be seen by others (television, the press or social media) is not true worship at all. It's all in the motive and God is concerned with underlying and secret intentions of the heart. We may think we are at peace with God when we do good, but if these actions are merely to appease a conscience, we are not truly at peace with God. And if our charitable endeavours smack in the least of conscience-appeasing or of making myself feel better, then our efforts are not transparently real and we cannot really be a peacemaker to those on the receiving end of our charity.

By way of example, when I clear out my cupboards, I piously put to one side bundles for the poor, for The Salvation Army, or some such charity. I grumble about going out of my way to find a suitable container to take all this stuff and then when I reach the bank I throw it in gaily. Having done my duty, I give myself a big tick for doing my bit. Really I am relieved to have relieved my wardrobe of too many items. Am I truly at peace with God and the poor at this moment? Probably not. I am rather glad Jesus was not waiting at the bins, discerning my heart, or that

I do not have to meet a real person in need and actually engage face-to-face with their troubles. However, from time to time, an envelope finds its way to a charity for the homeless – this time there has been a sacrificial gift of money; it has cost me. I feel it and I sense that this is true worship, pure fire.

## Jesus

Jesus' instructions were to render to Caesar what was Caesar's and to God what was God's (Mark 12:17). He told Peter to catch a fish and in its mouth was a coin, sufficient for both their taxes (Matt. 17:24–27). And his supreme gift was indubitably that of giving: giving to others in preaching, in miracles, in prayer, in prophecy, in healings, in friendship, and finally in the sacrifice of his life. Jesus' life was an altar of fire to his Father.

## Benefits

What we have discussed in this chapter is the exercise of strenuously working those flabby, atrophied spiritual muscles of service to God and others. Any alternative is abhorrent: Christian spiritual beings self-absorbed in their own personal piety, walking in impure fires of their own making, immune to the cries of the world or to ways of helping others. We would be no better, no different than our worldly peers. As disciples in Jesus' wake we are aiming to be turned-out towards the world and not away from it.

Mother Teresa told a reporter once that women came from all over the world to work with her on the streets of Kolkata (Calcutta) because they wanted to do something for others that was terribly hard. They wished to be taken to a place of extreme difficulty. They wanted a challenge. Isn't that interesting? And isn't it interesting that Mother Teresa herself devoted time each morning to the adoration of the cross affixed to her wall, the crucified Christ crying out 'I thirst'? In this prostrate figure, who modelled for a wealthy West a way of simple poverty, we find the entwined arms of the cross: the horizontal to others and the vertical to God – a sacrifice of pure fire, a peacemaker.

## Who will go with me?

There are two ways of looking at this: on the one hand, do not let your right hand know what your left hand is doing; and on the other, do to others what you would like done to you. The first practice has to do with our inner barometer: I alone know where my money or talent is going and I am responsible for making sure that I am on track with giving. This is mine and no one else's business. And that's well and good and excellent when it comes to remaining humble in the eyes of God (as we have discussed above). In this case, my prompt and nudge-giver is the Holy Spirit, who can invade and sensitise my conscience to keep my promises to God and neighbour.

However, keeping short accounts with the second practice of doing good to others may require more than my own eye upon myself: I am not always an accurate judge of my actions. It is at this point that I might consider talking to someone else, a worthy friend or soul-friend or even a spiritual director. I ask this person to hear me out about my concerns. I lay before them my inner struggle or anxiety. I ask them to pray with me. I go back to them after a while and seek their counsel again. I try to do what we have discussed and prayed through. I monitor the movements of my soul and adjust my actions with the help of the Holy Spirit. I rejoice exceedingly when I see that I am winning, and, when it seems I'll never ever get there despite all the help, I rejoice anyway, although I may choose to seek out some much-needed healing for a persistent problem when it comes to the gift of giving. And that is the subject of another treatise so enough said!

## Working out in disciplined devotion

Giving financially and giving in service to others are not optional extras in the life of the Christian. These disciplines are to become a lifestyle and we need to learn how to exercise them.

### Step one

First we accept that Christianity is not a religion with rules and regulations, but a relationship with a Father who desires that we become good children as he is good. And it is his good Spirit who makes us good and helps us to give voluntarily of our time, money and efforts for the kingdom of God. Anything else savours of legalism. Come to the altar of your heart in prayer and worship Jesus who gave it all up to God. Then try to give over your time, talents and resources to a loving Father. List them, name them, hand them over and ask the Holy Spirit to assist you to become a good giver.

### Step two

As you go on your way to make your offering of money or service, check out the state of your heart with God. Is there unfinished business with anyone? Are your motives for this deed completely pure or is there a tad trumpeting going on? Resolve there and then *before* you go, to make amends, to sort out your attitudes and to present a *good* sacrifice to the LORD. Then go ahead to do what you have resolved.

## Step three

Let's talk tithes and offerings. The Jews viewed money as integral to their worship of Yahweh. Tithes and offerings were mandatory in the Old Testament. As we have seen, Jesus was curious about how and what people gave, and the New Testament does not shy away from money but follows in the old ways of giving. For two thousand years, the Church has followed suit and disciples of Jesus have to work out how much, when and how. Traditionally, the minimum is a tithe (10% of net income) to the church. Then offerings in kind (food banks or clothing etc.) or offerings financial (charities etc.) are additional and up to individual conscience.

# WORKOUT EIGHT

## Persecution and worship

In this our final Workout, we turn once more to the art of Ancient Greek athleticism. The training regime in the gymnasium focused on a holistic ideal: a crop of healthy bodies and souls to yield a harvest of mentally and physically fit citizens and thus an invigorated body politic and state. Incorporated into this heroic mix was the aesthetic aspiration of the pursuit of the arts, and music in particular. The education of a 13- to 19-year-old boy included practising flute music to learn timing and grace – and running in heavy armour to the music of the flute. Music was believed to improve coordination. A long-jumper, body naked and oiled, would hit the track to the calming, soothing strains of flute music. Certain contemporary athletes employ music as it is considered a distraction, a motivational tool. At the start-up to the Olympics, trumpeters and singers entertained the great crowds of spectators until their competitiveness led to the their own contests at the games.

At the heart of the quest for excellence in the charioteers, wrestlers, boxers, runners, discus throwers and so on was the desire to be the finest and to attain immortality, a seat with the gods. To this end they competed and excelled and perfected their skills. The whole thing was worship and celebration of beauty and expertise and the winning athletes were crowned with glory and honour and praise.

All these heady excitements may seem far removed (and pagan) from the day-to-day pressure of following Jesus as an ordinary Christian. I was amused recently by a group of middle-class women in flowing trousers and sandals, a young male at their head beating a type of drum, striding out in the midday heat around a circle of standing stones. They were intense and engrossed and worshipping the place, the stones, the very air itself. Perhaps Christians need to wake up to a fresh anticipation of worship – its meaning and design – or else the pagans might win the garland!

Our present apathy may have less to do with the fact that a global pandemic has blocked normal church worship most successfully (that done in buildings), and more to do with the fact that the Western Church has had it too easy. Bring on a bit of persecution, like an anti-Christian repressive regime, and we might get back our fervour. There is nothing like opposition to spur and incite worship, albeit done in secret, despite the powers that be.

I recall listening to a Chinese pastor speak at a great gathering to celebrate the fall of the Iron and Bamboo Curtains. To a completely silent audience he told of his incarceration in a Communist labour camp and of his eagerness to be the lone prisoner marched each day to the human cesspool outside the camp. There the guards abandoned him to his task – the treading down of the human waste – each day for 17 years. The pastor's face shone and his thin body seemed magnified as he sang his song to us, the song from the pit, the old Methodist hymn, *In the Garden*:

*And he walks with me, and he talks with me,*
*And he tells me I am his own;*
*And the joy we share as we tarry there,*
*None other has ever known.*
(C. AUSTIN MILES, 1913)

I do not think there was a dry eye. We were

astounded and confounded by the simplicity of worship under the brutal yoke, under the cross of Christ. Such a champion was that pastor and what a garland he will wear in eternity. The pastor's cesspool became a pleasurable garden, a trysting place for the Beloved and the Lover. Tyranny turned on its head to a truce with God to bring a reward of blessedness under extreme persecution.

## Eighth beatitude

'Blessed are those who are persecuted because of righteousness, for theirs is the kingdom of heaven. Blessed are you when people insult you, persecute you and falsely say all kinds of evil against you because of me. Rejoice and be glad, because great is your reward in heaven, for in the same way they persecuted the prophets who were before you' (Matt. 5:10–12).

In this the final bit of the Beatitudes we come to the toughest, the most testing of these teachings. The central word in the text is one we discussed in the fourth Workout, the word *dikaiosunē* (righteousness). God makes us right with Christ through his saving action on the cross. God's justice helps us to safety out of Satan's grip. This kind of justice or right action is from divinity itself; it is the gift of God to us and belongs to those who call themselves children of God because they have entered the circle of Jesus' disciples. The 'righteous' are those who belong, in the first instance, not to the world, but to Christ. The persecutions they suffer, therefore, is because their allegiance is to him.

A woman I knew became a Christian. Her husband was so incensed at her new devotion to Christ and especially to her new set of lively church friends, that he took a job in another town to move her away. This subtle form of persecution had absolutely no effect on her faith, which remained as robust as ever, and reluctantly he was forced to admit defeat and moved back to the town and the lively church fellowship.

Jesus is telling his close friends: Watch out for the coming troubles, because troubles are inevitable for my followers. When you are spoken against, lied about, encounter hostility and so on, be glad! You belong to me and your future is a joyful one.

## Worship and celebration

I do believe that praise and worship is at the heart of Christian discipleship. Without it we dry up, become only cerebral, less powerful and less connected to the source of divine life. As we have seen in the previous chapter, our whole life is an offering to God. However, when we physically open our mouths to sing, to chant, to pray out loud, to rejoice in hymns ancient and modern, and in tongues, we join the perpetual worship of heaven – those who have gone before, the celestial choirs and the elders and living creatures. Let's be quiet and orderly with mouselike murmurings. Nothing wrong with that. But we can also be noisy and exuberant and wildly extravagant – as though we were at a rock concert or football match. Whatever our worship looks like it is better to do it than not to do it, not because it makes us feel better (although it certainly has that effect) but because it is the first commandment: Worship the LORD your God with all our heart, soul and strength.

*So how shall we understand the actual practice of celebration and worship as a spiritual discipline? Is this something done alone, or in groups or only in church services or meetings?* Any one of these ways and all of them, too. We are told to rejoice evermore and pray without ceasing – presumably as an individual on one's own, mostly. And this is an act of will, to turn in the dawning light to God as our first thought, to switch off the light with God as our last thought, to decide for praise rather than a grumble, to sing aloud and to give thanks.

But we are also instructed not to absent ourselves from the believers' gatherings, not to stop meeting together as a church. Thus corporate worship is a spiritual discipline as it means joining fellow Christians whether we feel like it or not, like them or not, whether the preacher pleases us or not, whether the songs are too old or too current. We all have our preferences, but the command to worship overrides our consumer mentality – picking the church best suited for us – because worship is not about us, it is all about him. And if this is a pill too hard to swallow, consider the multiplication of denominations, the plethora of beliefs through the years. How do our hardened differences strike an unbelieving world? Will it be drawn and converted to people at loggerheads? Does it really matter all that much whether the minister is robed or suited, kneels or sits to pray, genuflects or claps vigorously, waves incense or blows a shofar?

Worship is an act of homage and surrender to God. Perhaps that is why it is so contested and why it is a battle. Matt Redman, a songwriter and musician, in his song *We Praise You* calls us to arm ourselves with praise, using it as a weapon against the enemy.

## Jesus

We see the battle lines drawn over worship in Jesus' contest with the devil in the desert. At the third temptation to bow down and worship Satan, Jesus declares, '"Worship the LORD your God, and serve him only." Then the devil left him.' (Matt. 4:8–11). Did Jesus worship? That he did. On one occasion he was so filled with joy that he danced in his spirit and, speaking to his heavenly Father, thanked him for revealing his purposes to the poor and unlearned disciples who had come back rejoicing from a mission trip of healing and delivering from evil spirits (see Luke 10:21).

## Benefits

During the pandemic, there was a time when I experienced a certain 'flatness' with the ongoing global situation and the cutting back of meeting together for worship, work or socialising. I knew I had to get over the hump before the hump blocked my view of God. But what to do to get back my mojo, my chutzpah – that audacity and cheek to drive my life whatever the prevailing climate?

An understanding friend prayed for me

overnight, and bright and early I rose, chose a thunderingly good faith-filled set of worship tracks, attached my phone to my arm, my headphones to my ears, my trainers to my feet and set off on a five-mile run on Roundway Down. It felt significant to be on the site of a strategic battle in the English Civil War fought in 1643. I had my own battle. As I worshipped in the early morning light, battling a 29-kilometre wind on the homeward stretch, I felt Jesus come right alongside me and in my heart of hearts experienced a new power and decisiveness. I was over the hump.

## Who will go with me?

The first obligation in a workout routine in praise and worship is to the state of our own souls.

*Why, my soul, are you downcast?*
*Why so disturbed within me?*
*Put your hope in God,*
*for I will yet praise him,*
*my Saviour and my God.*
(PSA. 43:5)

If we find that we are not enjoying a hopeful and upbeat communion with our LORD then we need to speak to our souls as the psalmist instructs. Come on now, O soul of mine, cheer up, look up, thank the LORD and praise him. And if that is a temporary solution only and we keep slipping back into gloom and doom, we need to keep doing it, keep re-training our souls so that praise becomes a permanent state. For this we require the Holy Spirit. We can pray: Come, Holy Spirit, fill me and lift me to God in praise. Then we can put on a song, be it a streaming site or CD – whatever works – and praise. Work on it!

And the second obligation is the help and support of fellow Christians. Meet often and simply pray and worship. Go to a church building on Sundays if you can and take Holy Communion, say the psalms, hear the readings, listen to a talk and sing your heart out with others. For it is here with one another that we experience the fellowship of the Holy Spirit, that *koinōnia*. This word comes from the Greek word, *koinos* (common). *Koinōnia* is that which we have in common. When we find our Christian ideas are at enmity with the rest of the world, we run to the fellowship, to find our commonalty with fellow believers. When we are persecuted for righteousness' sake we can be untroubled because we belong to the body of Christ and our identity is not in the world but from the Father.

## Working out in worship

To craft a habit of worship and celebration is the best defence against the wiles of our enemy to bring us down, shut us up and confine us in misery. Here are three simple steps to get going and maintain a life of praise.

### Step one

Start with the goodness of God in private prayer each day. Give over a few minutes to celebrating his goodness by saying a psalm of thanksgiving, or singing a hymn or chorus, or singing in tongues, or by worshipping to a song (or dancing to a song).

### Step two

Stop what you are doing several times during the day to tune in, to make a conscious attempt at praise and thanksgiving despite your circumstances.

### Step three

Sacrifice part of Sunday to attend a church service somewhere, either online/virtually or even better in a physical space. Or listen to a church service on the radio or television if you are unable to get out. But be there with believers.

# CONCLUSION

As you come to the end of this very short excursion into the spiritual exercises, you may be distinterested by it all, titillated to discover more, nerved to begin at once or cautiously and tentatively taking first steps. Whatever you do, resist the very real temptation to go on *reading* about spiritual direction. Once you do that you may never stop as this is a wide, wide field. Much as you may relish the study and revel in its length and breadth, thrilled by the sheer novelty and strangeness of newness, none of that is actually *doing* it. We must take the plunge and get stuck in to 'working out'.

Take the 'couch to five kilometres' programme for absolute beginners. The newbie has to start running straightaway, from 30 seconds to 45 seconds to 90 seconds to 10 minutes. And so on. There is no substitute for action here. No amount of reading about running will cut it. We have to pummel the air, shout at the wind, get settled, get started, get cracking and move! So, give it a go. Take a stab at it. Make a start. Build up your strength. Extend the kingdom.

Because, just like the Ancient Greek athlete – all for the honour of the name of the god – none of this is really for us. All is for the glory of God. Spiritual growth and wellbeing are just amazing by-products. As we work out in these practices, as we improve our friendship with the Saviour, as we grow in our knowledge of the LORD and his ways, so the kingdom advances little by little. And so the glory of God fills the earth. Jesus has no hands but ours to do his will, no feet but ours to walk his ways, no mouth but ours to sing his praise, no heart but ours to love him more. Athletes for Christ, arise!